JR. GRAPHIC FAMOUS EXPLORERS

Samuel de Champlain

Andrea Pelleschi

PowerKiDS
press.

New York

Published in 2013 by The Rosen Publishing Group, Inc.
29 East 21st Street, New York, NY 10010

First Edition

Editor: Joanne Randolph

Book Design: Planman Technologies

Illustrations: Planman Technologies

Library of Congress Cataloging-in-Publication Data

Pelleschi, Andrea, 1962-

Samuel de Champlain / by Andrea Pelleschi. — 1st ed.

   p. cm. — (Jr. graphic famous explorers)

Includes index.

ISBN 978-1-4777-0074-7 (library binding) — ISBN 978-1-4777-0133-1 (pbk.) — ISBN 978-1-4777-0134-8 (6-pack)

1. Champlain, Samuel de, c. 1567-1635. 2. Explorers—America—Biography. 3. Explorers—France—Biography. I. Title.

F1030.1.P45 2013

971.01'13092—dc23

[B]

2012020631

Manufactured in the United States of America

CPSIA Compliance Information: Batch #W13PK1: For Further Information contact Rosen Publishing, New York, New York at 1-800-237-9932

Contents

Introduction

Samuel de Champlain was a French explorer, mapmaker, and **geographer**. He began exploring North America when he was just a young man. He is probably best known as the **founder** of the settlement now known as Quebec City. He also gained fame because he explored the eastern Great Lakes and created the first accurate map of New France.

Main Characters

Samuel de Champlain (c. 1567–December 25, 1635) French explorer who founded the city of Quebec in Canada. Quebec was the first European settlement in Canada.

Pierre du Gua de Monts (c. 1558–c. 1628) Governor of Acadia and founder of the first permanent settlement in Canada. He was also an explorer and a **fur trader**. He paid for **expeditions** to Canada and, in return, received a **monopoly** on fur trading in all of Canada.

François Gravé du Pont (Pont-Gravé) (c. 1554–c. 1629) Fur trader and captain in the French navy. He took Samuel de Champlain on his first expedition to Canada in 1603.

Guillaume Hellaine (?–1601) Samuel de Champlain's uncle. He was a **navigator** and a navy captain. When he died, he left Champlain a fortune.

King Henry IV (December 13, 1553–May 14, 1610) King of France. A popular king, he is known for bringing unity and prosperity to France. He supported Samuel de Champlain's exploration of Canada.

SAMUEL DE CHAMPLAIN

SAMUEL DE CHAMPLAIN WAS BORN IN BROUAGE, FRANCE. HIS FATHER, ANTOINE, WAS A SEA CAPTAIN.

I WANT TO SEE THE NEW WORLD!

IT'S A GREAT OPPORTUNITY FOR A YOUNG MAN LIKE YOU.

AFTER REACHING SPAIN, CHAMPLAIN BOARDED A SHIP BOUND FOR THE WEST INDIES AND CENTRAL AMERICA.

DURING THE VOYAGE, CHAMPLAIN LEARNED HOW TO SPEAK SPANISH.

HOLA, SAMUEL. THAT MEANS "HELLO."

HOLA!

HE ALSO DREW MAPS AND PAINTED PICTURES OF THE ISLANDS.

YOU'RE DOING A GREAT JOB.

THANK YOU, SIR.

HE BECAME AN EXPERT NAVIGATOR.

THESE ARE EXCELLENT. YOU HAVE A GOOD EYE FOR DETAIL.

THANK YOU. I ENJOY THE WORK.

I WOULD LIKE YOU TO BECOME MY OFFICIAL GEOGRAPHER.

IT WOULD BE MY HONOR.

SOON AFTER ARRIVING HOME, CHAMPLAIN FOUND THAT HIS UNCLE GUILLAUME WAS VERY ILL.

I AM LEAVING YOU MY SHIP, MY HOUSES, AND MY LAND.

NO, DON'T TALK OF SUCH THINGS!

WHEN HIS UNCLE DIED, SAMUEL DE CHAMPLAIN BECAME VERY WEALTHY.

WHAT WILL YOU DO NOW?

I WOULD LOVE TO TRAVEL AND SEE MORE OF THE WORLD.

SOON, A FUR TRADER NAMED PONT-GRAVÉ PLANNED AN EXPEDITION TO CANADA. HE WANTED CHAMPLAIN TO COME WITH HIM.

I CAN USE YOUR MAPMAKING SKILLS ON MY TRIP.

IT SOUNDS EXCITING.

IN MAY 1603, CHAMPLAIN AND PONT-GRAVÉ ARRIVED AT THE MOUTH OF THE ST. LAWRENCE RIVER.

WELCOME TO TADOUSSAC. IT'S THE MAIN TRADING POST HERE.

IT'S BEAUTIFUL COUNTRY.

WHERE ARE WE GOING?

TO MEET WITH THE **MONTAGNAIS**. WE DO MOST OF OUR TRADING WITH THEM.

I HAVE HEARD FROM YOUR KING. HE SAYS HE WILL HELP US DEFEAT OUR ENEMY, THE IROQUOIS.

IT'S TRUE. WE WANT TO KEEP TRADING WITH YOU.

I AM GLAD TO HAVE YOUR KING AS A FRIEND.

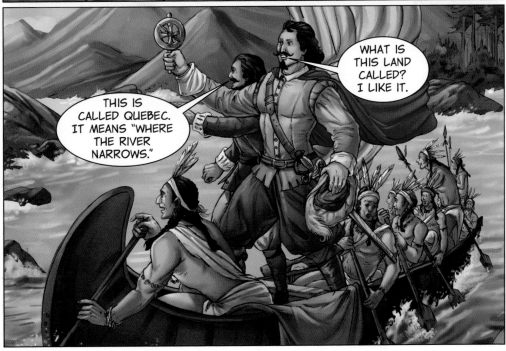

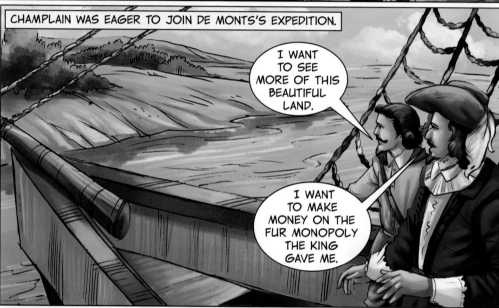

DE MONTS COULD NOT HAVE PICKED A WORSE LOCATION FOR THE SETTLEMENT.

THERE ARE SIX MONTHS OF WINTER HERE!

I DON'T KNOW HOW WE'LL LAST.

ABOUT HALF THE SETTLERS DIED THAT WINTER, SO DE MONTS ASKED CHAMPLAIN TO FIND A BETTER LOCATION.

IT LOOKS GOOD.

PORT-ROYAL HAS PLENTY OF FRESH WATER, AND THE SOIL IS BETTER.

CHAMPLAIN LIKED THE NEW LOCATION, AND A SETTLEMENT WAS BUILT AT PORT-ROYAL.

SOON, HOWEVER, RIVAL FUR TRADERS ARRIVED AND FORCED THE SETTLERS TO LEAVE.

WE'LL BE BACK SOMEDAY, SAMUEL.

I HOPE SO!

13

After surviving the winter, Champlain wanted to strengthen ties with the Montagnais. He also met with the Hurons and Algonquins.

Champlain and his Native American **allies** set off for Iroquois territory.

THEY SHOW A GREAT CALM.

BUT THEY ARE FIERCE FIGHTERS. BEWARE.

MORE THAN 200 IROQUOIS CAME OUT TO FIGHT CHAMPLAIN AND HIS ALLIES.

FIRE! THEY'VE NEVER SEEN YOUR THUNDER STICKS BEFORE.

DO NOT HESITATE!

YOU HIT THEIR CHIEFTAINS!

WE DID IT!

VICTORY!

FOR THE NEXT 18 YEARS, SAMUEL DE CHAMPLAIN WORKED HARD TO MAKE NEW FRANCE A SUCCESS. IN CANADA, HE TRIED TO KEEP HIS NATIVE AMERICAN ALLIES HAPPY.

YOUR PEOPLE MAKE GOOD TRADING PARTNERS.

AS PARTNERS, WE NEED YOUR HELP AGAINST THE IROQUOIS AGAIN.

THEY'RE TOO STRONG. WE CAN'T GET THROUGH THE WALL!

IN 1615, THE FRENCH AND THE HURONS ATTACKED THE IROQUOIS IN THEIR FORT.

BACK IN FRANCE, CHAMPLAIN FOUGHT TO KEEP PEOPLE INTERESTED IN CANADA.

CHAMPLAIN CONVINCED **MISSIONARIES** AND FAMILIES TO MOVE TO QUEBEC.

BY 1627, HOWEVER, THERE WERE FEWER THAN 70 PEOPLE IN QUEBEC.

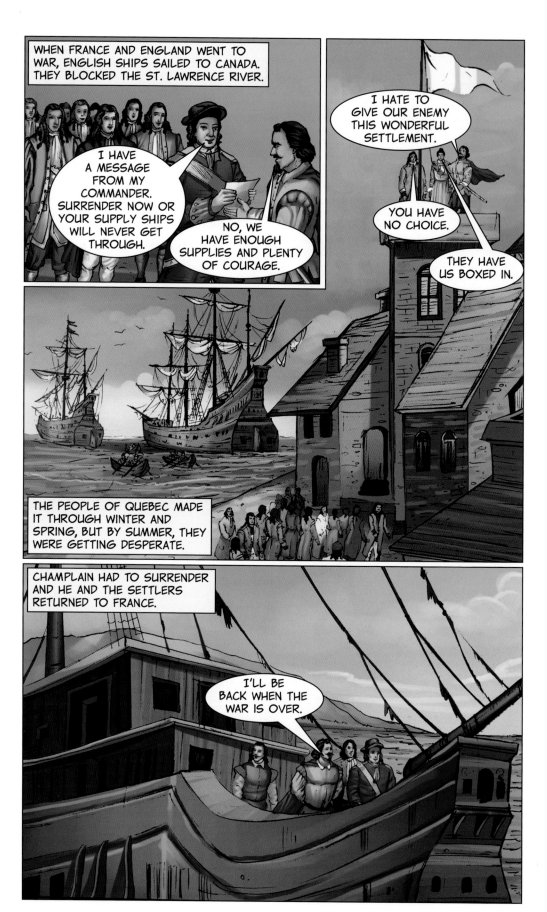

Timeline and Map

c. 1570	Samuel de Champlain is born in Brouage, France.
1603	He travels with Pont-Gravé to Canada for the first time. He sees the land that will become Quebec.
	He writes and publishes a book about his travels called *Des Sauvages*.
1604–1607	Champlain helps build the Saint Croix and Port-Royal settlements.
July 3, 1608	He founds Quebec along the St. Lawrence River.
July 30, 1608	He joins the Montagnais, Huron, and Algonquin Native Americans in fighting the Iroquois near Lake Champlain. They win the battle.
1613	Champlain travels west by canoe and explores the area west of Quebec. He travels up the Ottawa River.
1616–1624	Champlain tries to generate more interest and support for Quebec but has little success.
1627	England and France go to war.
1628	English forces demand that Champlain surrender Quebec. He refuses.
July 19, 1629	Champlain finally surrenders Quebec to the English forces.
	They take him back to France, where he learns that the war is already over.
March 29, 1632	In a treaty with England, France regains control of Quebec.
1633	Champlain arrives back at Quebec to help rebuild the settlement.
December 25, 1635	Samuel de Champlain dies.

Map of Champlain's Routes (1603–1615)

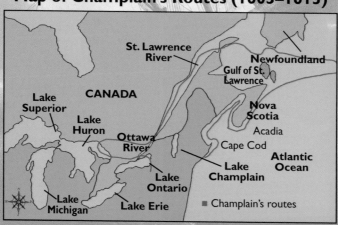

Glossary

allies (A-lyz) Groups of people or countries that are friendly and that help each other in times of crisis.

astrolabe (AS-truh-layb) An instrument that measures the positions of stars, used to find one's way on the oceans.

expeditions (ek-spuh-DIH-shunz) Trips for special purposes.

founder (FOWN-der) The person who starts something.

fur trader (FUR TRAY-der) A person who buys and sells animal pelts.

geographer (jee-AH-gruh-fer) A scientist who studies the features of Earth.

grant (GRANT) To give permission or allow something that was asked.

meager (MEE-ger) Very small in amount.

missionaries (MIH-shuh-ner-eez) People sent to do religious work in a foreign country.

monopoly (muh-NAH-puh-lee) A business owned by one group.

Montagnais (mohn-tahn-YAY) A French term meaning "mountain people." They are a group of Native Americans who lived along the north shore of the Gulf of St. Lawrence in Canada.

mutiny (MYOO-tuh-nee) A revolt of a ship's crew or of soldiers against their commanding officer.

navigator (NA-vuh-gay-ter) A person who uses maps, the stars, or special tools to travel in a ship, an aircraft, or a rocket.

opportunity (ah-per-TOO-nih-tee) A good chance.

quartermaster (KWOR-ter-mas-ter) An army officer who provides food, clothing, and other items for soldiers.

scurvy (SKUR-vee) A disease resulting from a deficiency of vitamin C, characterized by weakness and bleeding from mucous membranes.

seized (SEEZD) Attacked and took control of by force.

Index

Websites

Due to the changing nature of Internet links, PowerKids Press has developed an online list of websites related to the subject of this book. This site is updated regularly. Please use this link to access the list:

www.powerkidslinks.com/jgff/cham/